WHY YOU SHOULD BUILD DIGITAL SKILLS

Wants to Scale Your Income Results within a Short Time? Acquire Digital Skills

Glorioustina Essia

DISCLAIMER

TABLE OF CONTENTS

The Importance of Digital Skills in the COVID-19 Era

SECTION 4

The value of digital skills in today's workplace

Remote working and learning are becoming more popular.

Businesses are embracing digital practices.

Improve your skillset

Could help your employability

SECTION 5

10 Digital Skills That Will Make Students Employable in 2022

Use of social media

Search Engine Optimization (SEO)

Data Mining

Copywriting and Content Creation

Email marketing

Mobile Marketing

Digital Strategy and Planning

Social Media Marketing

Pay-Per-Click Advertising (PPC) (PPC)

Video / Podcasting

INTRODUCTION

Digital skills are essential. After all, technology's rapid evolution and rapid progress is omnipresent in our professional and daily lives.

It is safe to say that technology innovation has made us all more tech-savvy.

It is evident that the shift from traditional working methods to more digitally-focused workplaces is underway. Employers face a major challenge as they struggle to find qualified candidates for their digital skills.

These are just a few of the reasons digital skills are so important for you and your business. What might happen if you expect to get swept up in the digital revolution?

Digital skills are key to business productivity.

Competitive advantage: Digital skills are a must-have.

Digital skills can increase revenue and foster connections.

A company's online presence will be critical for increasing revenue as consumers move from high street shopping to e-commerce. Your website should allow customers to buy your services and also provide content that can be consumed by clients. This could lead to new business relationships or purchases. To increase revenue in a digital environment, you need to know your customers and be there. This requires a range of digital skills to engage, persuade and drive demand and loyalty.

Your bottom line is at risk if you are a digital laggard. Points of sale and payment processes, social marketing, content marketing, and social media - your clients, customers, and relationships are not where or how they used be. You must engage and find them on increasingly digital terms.

Digital skills are becoming more of a necessity than a luxury. It is important to take the time to learn about digital processes and to get the training you need to show the benefits of incorporating them into your daily life.

You will be able to embrace change and find new ways of doing business, which will increase productivity.

SECTION 1

What Exactly Are Digital Skills?

Digital skills, believe it or not, have been required for the workplace for decades. For as long as computers, servers, and electronic communications have existed, there has been a demand for digitally savvy professionals such as IT specialists and employees who can safely eject a floppy disk.

The ability to find, evaluate, use, share, and create content using digital devices such as computers and smartphones is referred to as digital skills.

Technology is central to our lives, and as our reliance on the internet and digital communications grows, our work ethics must evolve to meet the changing skill demand.

Why Should You Learn Digital Skills?

The rise of digital transformation is affecting every industry imaginable. Farmers are using sensors and information technology to automate, monitor, and regulate their systems in order to become more profitable, efficient, and sustainable. Food delivery apps assist restaurants in providing menu options to hungry customers without requiring them to leave their homes. This adds a new layer of complexity to restaurant workers' responsibilities, as they must now manage orders via digital devices as well as any in-person interactions. Even real estate, which has traditionally been a face-to-face industry, is relying on digital skills. Prospects looking to relocate can take advantage of virtual walk-throughs, and signing documents remotely with services like DocuSign is a quick and convenient way to finalize an agreement.

The mass shift to online business operations caused by the COVID-19 pandemic increased the demand for digital literacy and individuals who could assist traditional businesses in successfully transitioning to an e-commerce world.

There is no way to drive innovation and remain competitive without a strong command of digital skills. Employers are aware of this, so they prioritize candidates who can demonstrate their digital literacy. Employees can contribute to their communities, future-proof their careers, and explore a wide range of professional opportunities by improving their digital skills.

For you stand out in today and increase your chances of success in whatever career path you choose, remember that there are always new skills to learn and technologies to master.

The ability to carry out tasks such as:

- Communicating via email
- Researching information online
- Handling sensitive information in virtual ecosystems
- Safely using cloud-based collaboration tools such as Google Drive, DropBox, and Microsoft Teams are required as entry level in most workplaces today.
- Creating and managing spreadsheets and online documents

• Basic device management, such as connecting to the internet or installing software updates

• Screen sharing during a video call

• Using online calendars and managing your schedule efficiently (and possibly others on the team) are also advantages for an employee seeking employment in today's world.

What Are the Most Important Digital Skills?

Depending on your career path, you may require additional skills related to your specific role.

- Original content creation,
- E-commerce,
- Network and information security,
- UX/UI design,
- Digital marketing,
- Social media marketing, and
- Data analytics are all examples of digital skills in the workplace.

Also for the Entrepreneur or self-employed graduates or freelancer, skills like:

- Website and Funnel Building
- Presentation Skills
- Voice Mastery
- Copywriting
- Social Media Marketing
- Lead Generation
- Content Creation and Marketing

are some of the skills that will cause you to be outstanding in areas of your endeavors.

How to Build or Improve Your Digital Skills

Almost a third of the workforce lacks the fundamental digital skills that employer seek, implying that a large population of professionals requires reskilling. You can benefit from additional training if you want to improve your digital skills or if you want to enter the workforce with a strong resume. Here are some alternatives to attending a traditional four-year college or university for developing digital skills.

Self-Learning: We've talked about how technology is a part of our lives, so we should recognize how important it is in helping us learn. There is a vast amount of information available online on any topic you can think of, making basic skills easier to learn.

Online Courses for Free: For a more structured experience, consider free online courses that allow you to learn at your own pace at a slightly deeper level than self-learning. You won't get all of the advanced material you need to land your dream job, but it will get you started on the path to gaining basic knowledge and essential digital skills.

Certificate Courses: Universities and some certified Institute offer dedicated certificate programs that provide intensive, in-depth instruction to ensure students have the digital skills and training necessary to be hired in today's workforce and to be able to run their own businesses for entrepreneurs and freelancers.

Digital Skills Platforms: Platforms like LAP organizes digital skills trainings and bootcamps to its members to provide accelerated courses led by industry experts, as well as mentorship coaching to help them stand out in their jobs / chosen career paths and meet their financial goals.

The demand for digital skills will only grow, so if you need to learn quickly, there's no better time than now! The future has arrived. Let's do it together

Your digital skills will prepare you for the future of work.

According to a Gartner survey of business leaders, 80 percent intend to allow employees to work remotely at least part of the time after the pandemic, and 47 percent intend to allow employees to work from home full-time.

It is undeniable that remote working will play an important role in the future of work, and as the virtual workforce expands, so will the technology to support it.

Acquiring digital skills is critical to keeping up with the rise of remote working and the rapidly changing technological landscape.

According to experts, the demand for employees with basic digital skills will increase by 69 percent by 2030.

Understanding which digital skills are most relevant to you and your businesses is a great place to start when developing skill set.

Should You Learn Digital Skills?

It's easy to believe that if you're not in the tech industry, you don't need to improve your digital skills; however, this couldn't be further from the truth. Not only does digital skills training help you grow and become more effective in your workplace or businesses, but research shows that it also makes you marketable. Because:

- Acquiring digital skills can help you boost revenue and attain your financial goals.
- Because of your strong digital skills, you can build stronger customer and interpersonal relationships.
- Having a team with strong digital skills can provide you with a competitive advantage.
- New strategies and approaches to working and running businesses can be found through digital means.

Digital skills are essential for both organizations and individuals in the future of work. Improved productivity and effectiveness, as well as improved communication, are just a few of the many advantages of digital skills training.

Training in digital skills is more important than ever.

With remote work on the rise and technology ever-changing, it's critical to ensure that you are effectively trained on the tools, technology, and digital skills that will help you succeed whether you are in the office or at home. One of the most significant barriers to productivity for remote employees is a lack of digital skills and technological glitches.

What is the significance of digital skills?

Nearly everything we do these days requires some level of digital proficiency, furthermore, as technology continues to advance, integrate with our lives, and become an integral part of our daily work lives, this will only become more prevalent.

From the capabilities of our smartphone to the advantages of systems such as Alexa or Google, technology simplifies life. The internet of things is right around the corner. In a nutshell, we are becoming more interconnected. You can now control your heating, lighting, and even your washing machine from your phone. Manufacturers are currently testing fridges that alert you when you're running low on key items and "Dash" buttons (from companies like Amazon) that allow you to quickly re-order your favorite items.

Fundamentally, it comes down to an ever-increasing demand for the appropriate digital skills. It's also a bad idea to assume that everyone has the necessary digital skills.

The keyword here is "investment." Invest in digital skills right now. Teach people about the importance of digital skills, expose them to the digital world and empower them to learn these skills for themselves. There are a few easy steps you can take: –

1. Don't be afraid, to begin with, the fundamentals – it's all too easy to assume that everyone is digitally literate. However, once you've established a solid foundation, adding new skills on top becomes much easier.

2. Demonstrate what's new – get excited about topics like big data, the internet of things, virtual

reality, and the cloud. Again, understand what these terms mean and how they might affect you? More importantly, it will energize you through the art of the possible.

3. Understand your strengths and weaknesses, but never underestimate the power of true digital literacy.

SECTION 2

Digital Literacy Skills

What exactly are Digital Literacy Skills? "Digital Literacy Skills are the ability and know-how of digital skills in conjunction with critical thinking across the varied digital platforms and devices. Possessing digital literacy skills entails a combination of digital abilities, competence, knowledge, practical ability, research, digital learning, comprehension, evaluation, interpretation, creation, and communication. Digital Literacy Skills exist in the space between Digital Skills and Digital Literacies.

Why Are Digital Literacy Skills Important?

Digital Literacy Skills are extremely important in our increasingly digital world. Knowing how to use a computer is one thing, but learning and applying these skills can have a significant impact on your life.

So, What Is the Importance of Digital Literacy?

Here are some of them:

Online Learning Benefits from Digital Literacy:

We live in a world where if we don't know the answer to a question, we can simply Google it and get a variety of answers from various sources.

Today's fantastic learning opportunities are the result of the democratization of education via digital platforms. Anyone with a digital device and internet access can access a wealth of information to expand their knowledge base.

Digital Literacy Skills enable us to take an even more active role in our education and enable us to learn almost anything. With the COVID pandemic, online learning and the search for online courses have skyrocketed in recent months, demonstrating the value of e-learning and online education.

We can become lifelong learners because we have mastered basic digital literacy skills. Our ability to search for information, evaluate sources, and use critical thinking skills to assess information enables us to become lifelong learners through the use of digital tools.

Having a wealth of information available to us 24 hours a day, seven days a week is extremely powerful and will serve us throughout our lives as we take on different roles and pursue different interests.

You Have a Competitive Advantage if You Have Digital Literacy Skills:

With Digital Literacy Skill you become an extremely valuable asset to any company simply by learning and developing these skills.

Not only will having sought-after skills make it easier to find work, but it will also increase your income. Having such valuable skills allows you to command higher pay as a freelancer or while working for a company.

Many tech and non-tech companies are looking for skilled individuals with these in-demand skills, and they are willing to pay you fairly for the value you can bring to their organization.

Effective Communication is aided by digital literacy skills:

You can more effectively communicate ideas to your audience if you are familiar with various platforms, users, data analytics, and digital marketing principles.

People with digital literacy skills, for example, can use platforms like YouTube to create content for specific audience demographics to increase their awareness, subscribers, and even help drive sales conversions for products.

They can then analyze audience behavior and the effectiveness of their communication using analytics and data, and then take appropriate action to achieve their objectives. Digital Literacy Skills principles can be applied to jobs such as Search Engine Optimization (SEO), Digital Marketing, Advertising, UX/UI, Digital Strategy, and others.

Skills in digital literacy improve efficiency:

We've all heard the adage "Time is Money," and what better way to demonstrate that than through technological advancement?

We can now access information in seconds thanks to digital technology and platforms, saving us time and resources. Because of the nature of the online world, we can instantly connect with people on the other side of the world.

Man has invented inventions to help us communicate and stay more connected, such as the telephone, radio waves, television, and movies, always pushing the boundaries and innovating better, more efficient solutions.

From ordering a taxi from anywhere with internet access to saving lives through quick communication and response, technology has come a long way.

Digital Literacy Skills enable us to take the wheel and drive our digital devices to help us achieve our goals. The implications for businesses enable us to grow more quickly and connect with users all over the world.

Digital businesses have grown much faster than non-digital businesses.

Digital Literacy Skills Aid in Information Evaluation:

Because of their popularity and engagement, social media platforms enable us to reach a larger audience.

We gauge the success of our photos and videos by the number of views and likes they receive. It is one method of determining how well we reach our target audience.

Again, having digital literacy skills allows us to examine the vast array of digital platforms to use them efficiently to reach audience demographics. From social media to advertisements, SEO, SEM, YouTube, and more the ability to access massive amounts of information online is extremely useful in our daily lives.

Not all information, however, is created equal. This is where our Digital Literacy comes into play. Digital literacy skills enable us to evaluate and assess information using our critical thinking or digital literacies, assisting us in becoming more aware and responsible digital citizens.

We can use our critical thinking and reasoning skills to evaluate information sources, compare different sources of information, and arrive at our conclusions based on sound reasoning and judgment.

Misinformation, uncertainty, and knowledge-based on untrustworthy and weak sources can result from a lack of Digital Literacy Skills combined with limitless information.

Skills in Digital Literacy Are Crisis/Future Proof:

In 2020, the importance and relevance of Digital Literacy Skills was even more apparent. We were forced to quarantine due to the Covid-19 pandemic, and many of us had to learn to work from home.

Even those who weren't particularly "techie" found themselves on video calls figuring out the proper audio and video settings, as well as how to share information. This, however, should not have come as a surprise.

There have been numerous instances where people have been disrupted by technology. Aside from crises, disruption occurs whenever innovations are developed. Our ability to adapt quickly can help us thrive during times of transition.

Consider all of the factory workers who are laid off when a machine can do a better job. Consider recent examples of businesses such as Blockbuster that went bankrupt because they saw changes and refused to adapt to consumer needs, only to be surpassed by streaming services.

Individuals and businesses can use digital literacy skills to stay ahead of the competition and, in effect, Future Proof themselves.

They enable us to use technology to further our cause and provide solutions when traditional business models no longer function in a digital world.

Digital Literacy Skills Can Increase Your Income:

Having specific digital skills would earn you even more money. They also discovered an increase in demand for data analysis, digital marketing, and CRM.

Digital Literacy Skills Enable Creativity:

Digital Literacy Skills allow us to channel our creativity and imagination through digital devices and software designed to make our work better and more efficient.

We can bring our creations to life thanks to our digital literacy skills. From logo designs to Pixar films to fully interactive Virtual Reality Experiences, digital skills can help us expand our creativity.

All of the technology you use, apps you download, and websites you visit wcrc "crcatcd" in people's minds and realized through digital platforms.

Digital Literacy Skills Improve Security:

With so much of our lives documented on social media and so much information readily available, security is a very real concern.

Digital Literacy Skills enable us to navigate the internet with caution by allowing us to evaluate the information presented and be cautious of how and what we communicate online.

While many of us are aware that we should not give personal information to people or websites with whom we are unfamiliar, there are other ways in which our information can cause us harm.

Every action we take online, especially on social media, leaves a digital footprint. This information is easily accessible through a simple search and could be used against us.

Digital Literacy Skills enable us to use digital devices and the internet safely and responsibly, avoiding security risks, falling victim to online scams, and managing our digital footprint.

SECTION 3

The Importance of Digital Skills in the COVID-19 Era

The global pandemic of COVID-19 has altered how the world operates, highlighting the limitations of many existing systems and emphasizing the need to reimagine the role of information technology as a driver of economic productivity and growth. Countries have imposed mobility restrictions and, in some cases, lockdowns in an attempt to contain the virus, which has fundamentally disrupted the functioning of society and the economy. This disruption has altered how communities, businesses, and individuals operate, communicate, and share knowledge.

The measures and solutions adopted by governments and organizations in their efforts to maintain business and operational continuity are hastening the emergence of the fourth industrial revolution. The possibilities presented by the fourth industrial revolution are vast. Following the pandemic, organizations, businesses, and individuals hoping to capitalize on the fourth industrial revolution will need to reconsider their strategic approach to leveraging technology and digitalization. To prepare for the fourth industrial revolution, they will need to reposition technology as a critical component for each sphere of specialization, as well as learn the necessary digital skills to become creators and users of these tools.

Businesses and governments must digitize their operations and coordinate their activities to ensure business continuity and resilience in the face of future crises. Telecoms and media have been less affected by the pandemic than, for example, aviation and tourism, which have been impacted by anti-pandemic measures. Companies in less impacted industries are better positioned to continue operating as usual, especially if they use embedded digital channels and tech solutions as part of customer service and other business operations. Indeed, once the business climate improves in the post-COVID-19 world, many may claim a larger market share.

The rapid growth of virtual working platforms enables organizations to ensure that their workforces remain productive. This trend has the potential to reduce operating costs while also pointing to the future of work.

Technology is assisting in reducing global disruptions in many, if not all, sectors of the economy. In the finance sector, for example, mobile money solution has ensured that most financial transactions are processed, Mobile money technology has contributed to a reduction in the need for physical cash transactions, thereby limiting the spread of the coronavirus. Mobile health platforms that provide 24-hour access to doctors across all specialties in several countries havc maintained medical services, reducing the burden on overburdened health centers. By leveraging their existing technology-enabled logistics systems, e-commerce platforms such as Jumia, Konga, and Amazon have provided channels for consumers to buy necessities.

More than a billion students worldwide got stranded at home because schools were closed, and roughly three out of every four students experienced disruptions in their learning processes as a result of the pandemic. E-learning technologies have been adopted by governments and school administrations for homebound students. Kenyan, Egyptian, and Nigerian educational systems, for example, now make materials and programs more accessible through cloud services, radio, television, and social media platforms.

The development of digital skills is an important part of preparing for economic and social shocks like the COVID-19 outbreak. This is already being recognized in Africa, where acquiring digital skills can serve as a hedge against the risks of unemployment. This reality has prompted African youth to prioritize the development of these skills, which are available on globally accessible virtual learning platforms.

SECTION 4

The value of digital skills in today's workplace

Living in a digital age necessitates a high level of digital savvy, and as work environments change and more companies strive for an online presence, the importance of digital skills in the workplace rises to the fore. Technology is rapidly advancing and transforming business practices, which has unavoidably had an impact on how people work and, as a result, the skills that job seekers must now adapt. There's a 'digital skills deficit,' and the demand for these skills in the workplace is increasing.

In this section, we will look at how businesses have adapted to remote working and why they are changing their business strategies to accommodate technological advancements. We will also look at why job seekers and employees should pay more attention to how they can adapt their digital skills to not only improve their employability in the future but also expand their skill set in their current roles.

Remote working and learning are becoming more popular.

As we all know, many companies around the world have transitioned to a work-from-home structure, and some organizations are still adopting this new way of working with no plans to return. Learning to be digitally savvy and familiar with many new digital practices was, and continues to be, essential for the majority of people, and it still is!

Many aspects of work changed when the world shifted to remote working and limited face-to-face interactions, from communicating online with employees via video calls and real-time messaging software to relying more on websites and social media to stay in touch with customers. To keep up with technological advancements, employees must now be familiar with digital applications, online sharing platforms, and a variety of other electronic software.

Further education has recently welcomed digital learning, and the pandemic's impact has even caused some universities and colleges to shift to a completely digital study structure. Many educational institutions are now investing in digital transformation to improve online learning, allowing materials and resources to be available 24 hours a day, seven days a week, in addition to pre-recorded seminars and classes.

So, if you are considering furthering your education or even taking the next step in your current career, make sure you brush up on your digital skills to ensure you are ahead of the game.

Businesses are embracing digital practices.

Even before the global pandemic, many businesses from various sectors made digitalization a top priority. To remain competitive, organizations must constantly keep up with modern technologies, whether that means introducing new website developments, mobile advancements, or advancing certain in-house software.

This is because many digital practices bring numerous benefits to organizations, such as increased productivity, improved communication, and increased efficiency. Another advantage for businesses that use technology in their operations is the increased security it provides, reducing the possibility of viruses or cyber-attacks. Going digital can also encourage businesses to become more innovative and collaborate in new ways via new technologies. Companies take advantage of these new technologies by increasing brand awareness through website advancements and increasing business exposure through platforms such as social media. This digital customer journey is now more important than ever for businesses.

As a result, while businesses continue to focus on digital transformation and incorporate emerging trends into their business models, it emphasizes the need for the current and future workforce to do the same.

Improve your skillset

The job market has quickly become a highly competitive environment, and this is likely to continue for some time. Even if your current career goals do not require much digital expertise, there is no harm in becoming acquainted with certain practices or brushing up on new information that may benefit your career development in the future.

The great thing about learning digital skills is that they are now required in many career paths across a wide range of sectors, as more industries rely on digital advancement to support business success. Understanding digital practices, as a result, provides you with invaluable and transferable skills that are beneficial to these many lines of work, allowing you to be versatile in your professional skills and knowledge.

Could help your employability

And, even though working from home and on the go is second nature to some of us, there is a significant skills gap.

Applicants who acquire solid digital knowledge and skills may gain a competitive advantage when applying for jobs and may even set you apart from your competitors in a highly competitive environment. These abilities may be critical to your success in obtaining employment, whether you are based in an office or expected to work remotely. Possessing the necessary skills allows you to gain a deeper understanding of digital practices, allowing you to pick up specific tasks quickly and be more efficient in the workplace, among other advantages.

As digital technology revolutionizes not only our personal lives but also our professional lives, it's time to put technology to work for you! Digital transformation is accelerating, and many more industries are adapting to technological change, emphasizing the importance of constantly honing our digital skills. Whether you are looking for your next job or considering a career change, now is the time to invest in your digital knowledge and focus on mastering a few new skills to spruce up your CV while contributing to personal and professional development.

SECTION 5

10 Digital Skills That Will Make Students Employable in 2022

Over the last decade, businesses of all sizes have digitized their operations and processes. Businesses are already using artificial intelligence (AI) to improve workflows and supply chains. As a result, today's job seekers must possess specialized skills to stand out from the crowd.

While some colleges, universities, and training providers have modified or expanded their curriculum to meet the growing demand for digital know-how, many educators are struggling to provide students with the necessary skills.

In this section, we reveal the ten most valuable digital skills that educators should provide to their students for them to land the top digital jobs across industries.

Students who learn digital skills not only increase their employability but also future-proof their careers by understanding key digital channels.

So, let's take a look at the top ten employable skills for students and employers.

Use of social media

A recent study found that there are over 4.2 billion active social media users worldwide. 4.15 billion of these are active mobile device users. These figures show a 13.2 percent increase in global social users in just one year, with no signs of slowing down.

Understanding and effectively using social media is a core and valued skill that every professional should have. Social media marketing is more than just sending out a tweet or updating your status on Facebook; it is about understanding the dynamic relationship between brands, influencers, and consumers. Simply put, businesses must reach out to customers to drive traffic to their website—or product—for potential conversion. It is now also important in providing good customer service, as many customers use social media to ask questions or make comments.

Search Engine Optimization (SEO)

Aside from social media, one of the most influential disciplines on which marketers have come to rely is Search Engine Optimization (SEO). To put things into perspective, 81 percent of internet users look for a product or service to buy online, with Google accounting for 70 percent of that traffic.

Students with SEO experience can use paid advertising to increase the visibility of a company's website on a search engine (e.g., Google or Bing). As a result, the company will receive valuable web traffic from search engine results pages.

Students will be able to capture valuable organic search traffic results by using SEO. That is why marketers, content managers, and webmasters spend so much time optimizing websites, especially for mobile and ad campaigns, to achieve the highest conversion rates possible.

Most businesses sell products or services and want to outperform their competitors to be easily found online. During the Covid-19 pandemic, the number of customers who went online to purchase increased, increasing e-commerce transactions. This means that job seekers with a working knowledge of search marketing will be extremely valuable to organizations in ensuring their visibility and searchability.

Data Mining

Data can provide a wealth of information to your students that, when used correctly, can result in effective marketing campaigns that drive conversions, sales, and revenue.

Data analytics essentially allows students to make informed, data-driven decisions that lead to better business insights. Numbers determine whether or not a campaign was successful and by how much. The key is to understand what data to collect and measure to improve the next campaign. Companies do not want to waste money on marketing based on trends or gut instincts. It is all about maximizing the effectiveness of each campaign and optimizing the return on investment.

Analytics and SEO go hand in hand, so these skills work together to ensure a company understands what its customers want and how to attract and retain their attention.

Copywriting and Content Creation

Blog posts, videos, podcasts, infographics, and even social media status updates are all examples of content.

Marketers may spend their time optimizing keywords and ad campaigns, but the content remains king. After all, the content on a website or social media page is what drives it, and without it, customers have no way of understanding the benefits of a product or service.

Content is critical for increasing brand awareness and positioning brands or influencers as thought leaders. As a result, new hires must understand the significance of creating content that is relevant to keyword research and optimizing it in a strategy. Students who gain experience and knowledge in content marketing will have valuable and employable skills that will prepare them for a career in any industry.

Email marketing

One of the most effective ways to acquire and retain leads is through a tried-and-true method: email.

Email is one of the oldest forms of direct marketing and continues to be effective in terms of customer acquisition and retention. From startups to multinational corporations, a solid email marketing strategy is essential for launching successful campaigns.

An experienced digital marketer understands that each funnel stage must be meticulously planned. Every step, from the signup page (including its placement on a website) to the welcome email, must be optimized to attract users and build engagement.

People may change their social media accounts or home addresses, but they rarely change their email addresses. As a result, experts who understand the power of email marketing to connect directly with customers are in high demand.

Mobile Marketing

Because smartphone traffic now outnumbers desktop traffic (64 percent), Google now employs mobile-first indexing when crawling pages and prioritizing content.

To understand the significance of this change, consider Google's creation of a mobile-friendly web app designed to test the usability and speed of mobile websites. Using mobile-friendly content can increase your search visibility among consumers who do not have access to desktop computers.

Job seekers can benefit from this knowledge by optimizing campaigns with the most recent advancements in mobile search and user expcricncc.

Digital Strategy and Planning

Businesses that use a digital marketing campaign strategy are more likely to see long-term measurable results. Instead of impromptu planning, digital marketers must create and implement campaigns based on analytics and quantifiable SEO data.

Setting specific KPIs and determining methods for measuring each indicator, for example, can assist a marketer in remaining accountable. It is also critical that they analyze previous campaigns and determine which metrics are worth measuring.

Educators should capitalize on this skills gap by teaching students how to plan and implement a digital strategy.

Social Media Marketing

Sales professionals must be where their prospects are: online, to connect with and influence them. Social Media Marketing is proving to be beneficial to sellers who use it; 65 percent rely on it to fill their pipelines, and it generates half of the revenue for 14 major industries.

Businesses are also starting to recognize the value of social media marketing by investing in new sales stack technology like email tracking tools, productivity apps, and sales intelligence software. Above all, social media marketing tools are regarded as highly effective in connecting with the modern buyer, who relies on social media for reviews and advice.

Pay-Per-Click Advertising (PPC) (PPC)

PPC is a popular way for brands to get quick traffic. Companies with large marketing budgets can have their search results appear on Google's first page, resulting in massive traffic. Google's AdWords program is a popular PPC advertising model, and using a PPC for eCommerce tracker is a great way to monitor spending.

Understanding impressions, reach, and cost-per-click is essential for the digitally savvy job seeker.

Video / Podcasting

Video has evolved from being just a form of entertainment to a major social media content driver. YouTube is now a powerful and influential platform while networks like TikTok and Instagram have turned the video on its head to create wealthy influencers.

Why is video so popular? With smartphone users becoming younger and younger, social media apps like WhatsApp, Weibo, and WeChat are becoming the de-facto tools of instant message communication. Indeed, WhatsApp has over 2 billion users worldwide.

Video content is more easily consumed than other formats, such as a blog post. It's also more enjoyable and appealing to Millennials. Markets can tap into a growing market of engaged consumers by combining the emotional power of social media video with the reach and scope of digital advertising.

www.ingramcontent.com/pod-product-compliance
Ingram Content Group UK Ltd.
Pitfield, Milton Keynes, MK11 3LW, UK
UKHW022009190726
13853UKWH00004B/1830